THE ATOMIC AGE

SCIENCE BOOK GRADE 6

CHILDREN'S HOW THINGS WORK BOOKS

BABY PROFESSOR

EDUCATION KIDS

The Atomic Age, which is also referred to as the
Atomic Era, is the time period that follows detonation
of Trinity, the first atomic bomb, on July 16, 1945,
which occurred during World War II.

THE ATOMIC BOMB

In 1929, at the beginning of World War II, the atomic bomb was not yet invented. It was during this time that scientists discovered that if they were able to split an atom, a powerful explosion might result. This bomb would be able to destroy cities in one blast and could change warfare in the future.

ATOMIC BOMB

ALBERT EINSTEIN

ALBERT EINSTEIN

Einstein had come up with several theories that scientists were able to use in creating this bomb. Once he realized that it could be made, he feared what might happen if Hitler was able to create the bomb first. He sent a letter to President Franklin Roosevelt of the United States advising him of his thoughts regarding the atomic bomb. Roosevelt then started the Manhattan Project.

While Einstein did not directly work on inventing the bomb, he is associated with it due to his scientific work as well as his discoveries were vital in the development of the bomb, particularly for his work on energy and mass and his well-known equation of E=mc2.

$$E = mc^2$$

While he had numerous discoveries, the Theory of Relativity is what he is most recognized for. In his Theory of Relativity equation, E=mc2, the "c" references speed of light and remains constant and is thought to be the quickest speed possible throughout the universe. The equation explains how energy (E) is related to the mass (m). This theory explains quite a bit of how distance and time are able to vary because of the "relative" or different speed of the observer, as well as the object.

MANHATTAN PROJECT

The Manhattan Project became the title for the development and research program for the bomb. It began as a small project, but one the idea seemed to be more realistic, the U.S. added more scientists as well as funding to make sure they had the bomb first. Several of the scientists involved in this project had left Germany. At the project's end, funding was at $2 billion and consisted of about 200,000 people involved in it.

OAK RIDGE SITE OF THE MANHATTAN PROJECT

FIRST ATOMIC EXPLOSION

Somewhere in the desert of New Mexico, the first bomb was set off on July 16,1945 and its explosion was huge and was equivalent to 18,000 tons of TNT and scientists believed the center temperature of this explosion was three times hotter than the sun's center.

While the scientists were pleased they had successfully created the bomb, they also became fearful as well as sad and fearful since it would probably bring change to the world and possibly cause death and mass destruction. Once President Truman became apprised of the success of the bomb, he penned "We have discovered the most terrible bomb in the history of the world".

HARRY S. TRUMAN

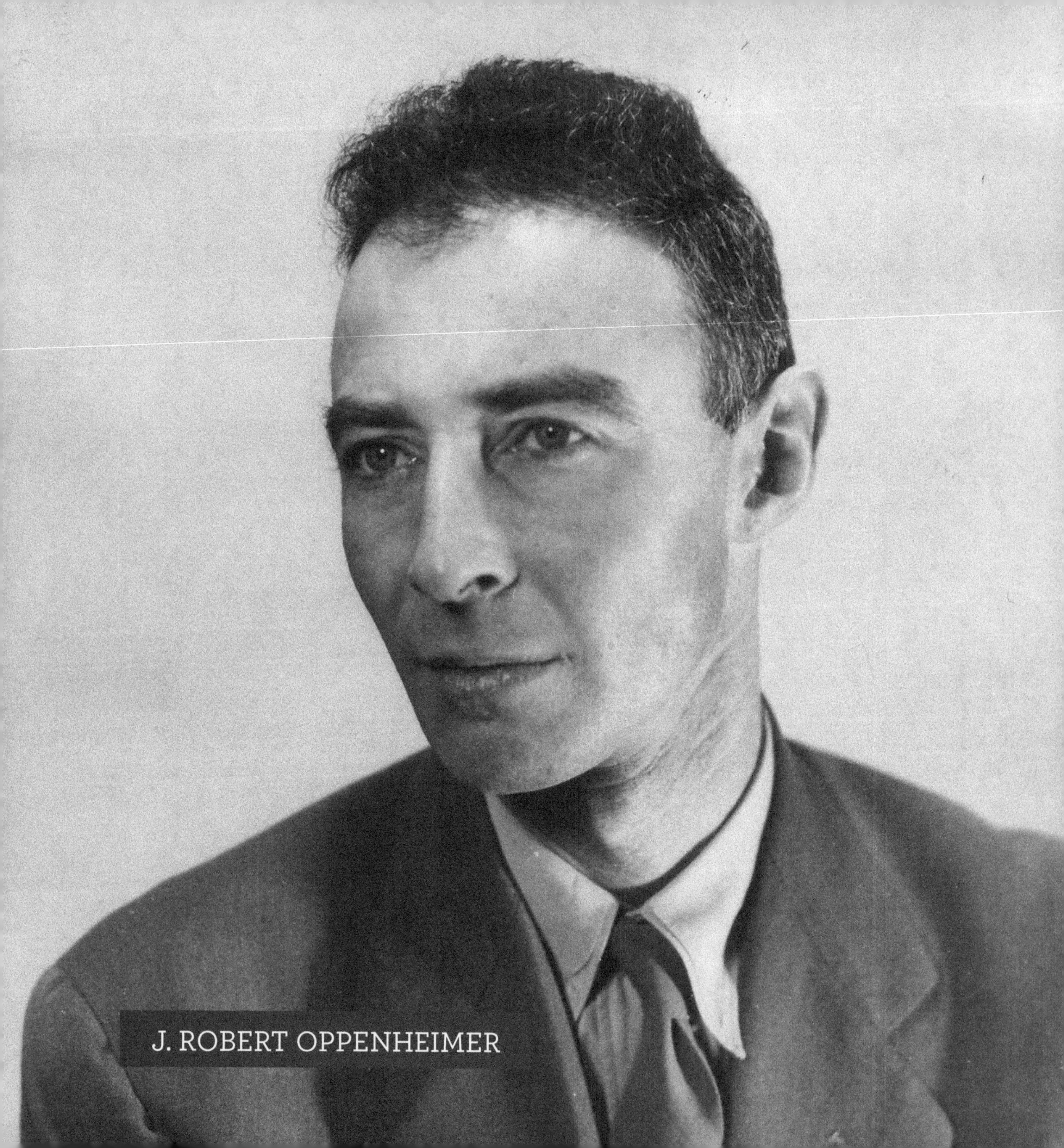
J. ROBERT OPPENHEIMER

J. Robert Oppenheimer was the lead scientist on this project and often is referred to as the "father of the atomic bomb".

THE DECISION TO DROP THE BOMB

Germany had surrendered and WWII was over in Europe when the first bomb was created. Japan had been defeated but refused to surrender. The United States was now thinking about invading Japan. The leaders of the Army believed that as many as 500,000 to 1 million U.S. and Allied soldiers would be killed during an invasion and President Truman chose to instead drop the atomic bomb.

ATOMIC BOMB "LITTLE BOY"

HIROSHIMA AND NAGASAKI

The atomic bomb referred to as Little Boy was dropped onto Hiroshima, Japan on August 6, 1945. There was a tremendous explosion that destroyed the city and killed thousands. It was dropped by an airplane known as the Enola Gay, piloted by Colonel Paul Tibbetts. The atomic bomb was more than 10 feet long and weighed approximately 10,000 pounds.

Hiroshima had been chosen since it was a city with a large port as well as an army base. In addition, it had not received much damage from the previous bombings. This showed just how strong this new weapon was.

HIROSHIMA BOMB
EXPLOSION

ATOMIC BOMB "FAT MAN"

Emperor Hirohito and Japan were still refusing to surrender even after seeing the horrible destruction from the bombing of Hiroshima. A second atomic bomb, referred to as Fat Man, was dropped on Nagasaki, Japan on August 9, 1945 and the devastation again was horrible.

The original bomb that was dropped on Hiroshima consisted of uranium. That bomb that was used on Nagasaki consisted of plutonium, which was more powerful than the uranium used in the bomb on Hiroshima.

NAGASAKI BOMB EXPLOSION

RUINS OF NAGASAKI ATOMIC BOMB

It is believed that as many as 135,000 lives were lost as a result of the Hiroshima bombing and 70,000 in Nagasaki. Several of these lives lost were civilians, including children and women.

SURRENDER

Emperor Hirohito and Japan finally surrendered to U.S. forces six days later. When the Emperor made this announcement on the radio, it was the first time most of the Japanese had ever heard him speak.

IMPERIAL PALACE GROUNDS IN TOKYO, JAPAN, IN 1945

WORLD WAR II

AFTER WORLD WAR II

After the end of WWII, things changed. Most of Europe as well as Eastern Asia was destroyed from the bombings and fighting that occurred over the years and several borders of various countries had to be set as well as re-establishment of governments where Japan or Germany had taken over.

EUROPE

During WWII, Germany occupied most of Europe and several countries of the west returned to their previous governments and borders. Germany, however, became separated in two parts, Western and Eastern Germany.

GERMAN TANKS

GERMAN SOLDIERS INVADING POLAND

Russia (USSR) controlled the east and the Allies controlled the west. In addition, the USSR took over several countries located in Eastern Europe where they battled with the Germans, including Romania, Poland, Albania, Bulgaria, Czechoslovakia, and Hungary.

Europe was in desperate need of financial aid since the bridges, roads, buildings, and much more were destroyed. The U.S. provided aid in the form of the Marshall Plan to assist Europe with its recovery.

220
220
1000
418
1415
1265
1049

EASTERN ASIA
AND JAPAN

Japan was now occupied by the Allies and the United States who maintained control while Japan was recovering from the war. In 1952, Japan became independent once again.

The USSR and the Allies divided Korea into North Korea and South Korea. The plan now was that Russia would control North Korea and the Allies would control South Korea until the entire country was able to hold a free election.

DALIAN
NORTH KOREA
KOREA
SEOUL
SOUTH KOREA
BUSAN

This election never took place since Russia would later refused and Korea remains split and communists control North Korea.

A civil war that began before WWII, between the nationalists and the communists, continued to take place in China. The communists would go on to win and the nationalists then left for Taiwan.

WAR CRIMES

Following WWII, several leaders from Germany and Japan were brought to trial for violating rules of war set forth by the Geneva Convention and they also had perpetrated crimes against humanity. Included in these crimes were slave labor, the Holocaust, and the horrendous treatment of prisoners of war, including torture. Several of these leaders were then executed for these crimes.

UNITED NATIONS

On October 24, 1945, The United Nations was formed by the Allies in an attempt to prevent World War III from taking place. Included in the 51 original nation members were five permanent Security Council members: France, China, the Soviet Union, the United States, and the United Kingdom.

UNITED NATIONS BUILDING IN GENEVA

BUNKER FROM COLD WAR

THE BEGINNING OF THE COLD WAR

There was an extended period of conflict between the communist countries of Eastern Europe and the Western World, which was known as the Cold War. The U.S. led the west and the Soviet Union led Eastern Europe and the countries became to be known as superpowers.

The Cold War began in 1945, not long following the end of WWII. While the Soviet Union was known to be an important member of the Allies, there was a lot of distrust between them and the remaining allies. The Allies became concerning about the brutal leadership under Joseph Stalin and the spread of communism. In 1991, with the Soviet Union collapse, the Cold War was now over.

FLAG OF THE SOVIET UNION

PEACE LOVE WORLD

The phrase "Atomic Age", while originally was used in a futuristic connotation, by the 1960s, threats of nuclear weapons was starting to have the advantage over nuclear power as the prevailing motif of the atom.

For additional information about the Atomic Age and World War II, you can visit your local library, research the internet, and ask questions of your teachers, family, and friends.

Visit
BABY PROFESSOR
EDUCATION KIDS
www.BabyProfessorBooks.com
to download Free Baby Professor eBooks
and view our catalog of new and exciting
Children's Books